THE ETERNAL GAME

CARDS ILLUSTRATED BY:
MAHAM AZIZ

CARDS DESIGNED BY:
S.E. WILSON & MAHAM AZIZ

SACRED GEOMETRY & MAP ILLUSTRATED BY:
ANJALI SINGH AND CARMA NAUDÉ

STORY BY:
S.E. WILSON A.K.A "EXQUIL"

TYPESET BY:
ALICE HUNT

Thank you so much for supporting The Eternal Game illustrated card deck. We have worked exceptionally hard to bring our visualisation of the conspiracy of Nephilem children to a reality. This final product was truly a labour of love an intellect.

We wanted these illustrations to serve not only as an introductory puzzle but also as art work that defines the aesthetic you will come to understand is the larger conspiracy of The Nephilem, the debut novel in the proposed series of The Eternal Game books.

The illustration deck invites you to map out, in the correct formation, the key players, and important symbology of The Eternal Game. This guide used as a companion to the novels will also help readers gain insight into the functions characters in the books will play.

Thank you and enjoy!

Ezquil & Maham Aziz and Carma Naudé

Table of Contents

ABOUT THE CARDS

The cards were made to help you gain deeper understanding of the conspiracy of Nephilem children known as The Eternal Game. The illustration deck invites you to map out, in the correct formation, the key players of The Eternal Game. If you pay attention to small details of iconography and symbolism and deft use of connotations, you will also gain an insight into the functions characters play in the conspiracy of the proposed book series.

The deck comprises of 13 cards. Each card has been painstakingly designed individually but also has elements that bind it to at least one other card in the deck and in a few cases, many other cards.

Developing the concept of The Eternal Game deck had been carefully planned over a long amount of years, but the illustrations have been crafted organically and initiatively at the fingers of the illustrator in just over 6 months.

Maham followed each design and interpreted them into her own fascinating vision, pouring her passion for the project into ensuring warm colours mixed together from one set of cards to the other. Each card is intricately layered, engineered with symbolisms, imbued with mysticism and channelled with motifs that gives you messages about the type of people involved in the conspiracy of Nephilem children which is at the heart of The Eternal Game series of proposed books.

ABOUT THE
ETERNAL GAME

The Eternal Game, though pictorialized through tarot-style cards, is not a game or a tarot at all, but a record of thoughts and deeds carried out in the name of Nephilem. These thoughts and deeds are held by the *Circle of Judges* who are stewards of the *Sacred Mystery, The Akashik,* also known as The Blanket of the Stars. The *Circle of Judges* often assign a mystagogue to initiate the *burden bearer* of The *Akashik*.

How thoughts and deeds are recorded on The Blanket of the Stars is a *Sacred Mystery*, and in this sense cannot be explained or apprehended by reason alone. Thus, it is mystical and awaits disclosure or interpretation revealed by God.

The Eternal Game records thoughts and deeds of: Nephilem, Traders, Collectors, Hunters, Protectors, Enemies and the Burden Bearer of the Akashik. Enemies of the Nephilem are classified in two schools: Owls and Crows. These are eternal enemies since the beginning of time, and will attempt to attack or kill each other with an instant dislike. Diametrically opposing Owls and Crows are Protectors.

However, Protectors, Owls and Crows are unknown variables in The Eternal Game. Everyone in The Eternal Game is classified either as a *Protector* or Enemy of the Nephilem; even *Nephilem* themselves and *Hunters*. One tends to align themselves to protect their position in the game given the situation.

LAYING OUT YOUR CARDS

If you look carefully at the cards you may have already noticed a thematic colour theming. This was designed to give you a sense of the economy at stake and its partnerships in The Eternal Game.

When attempting to use the accompanying poster to layout the cards in formation pay attention to minor details found in the cards to bring along your solution. We are hoping this interaction with the cards will bring about a community spirit by means of discussion about the conspiracy of The Eternal Game and how the first book, The Nephilem, sits underneath its umbrella.

INTRODUCING THE CARDS

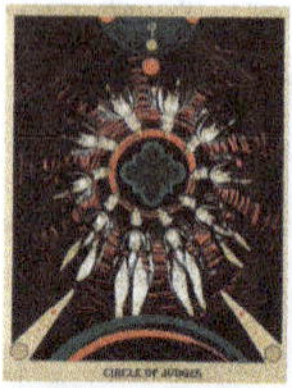

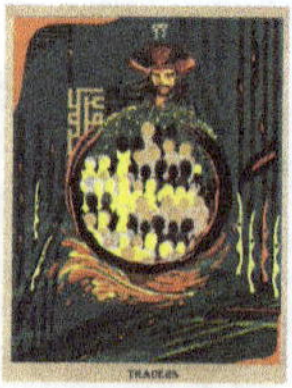

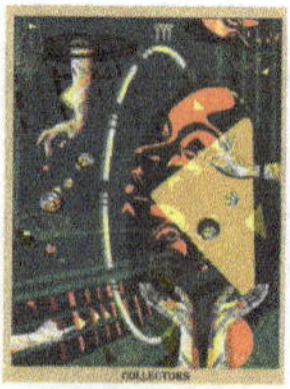

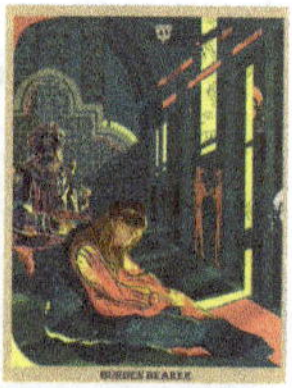

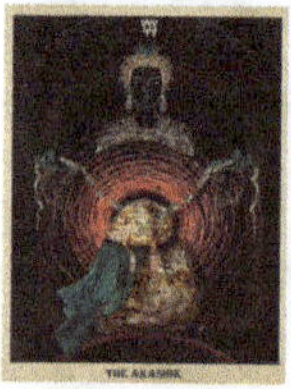

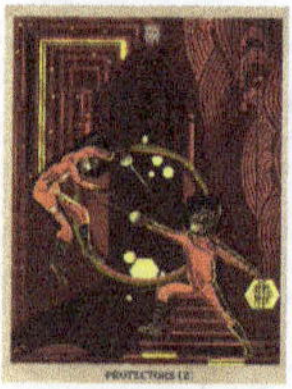

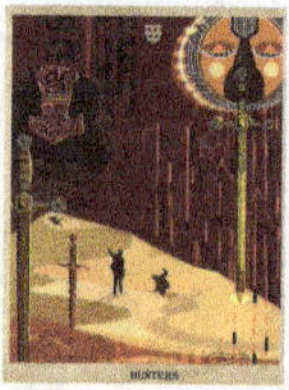

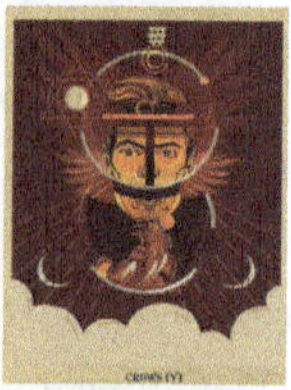

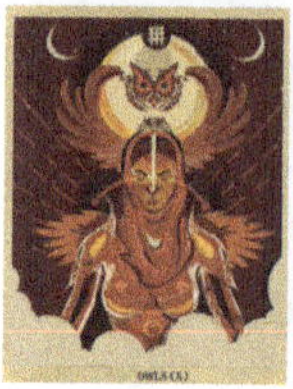

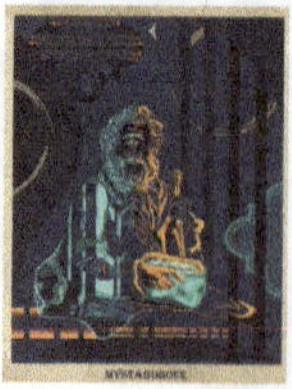

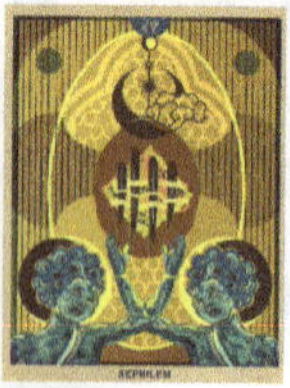

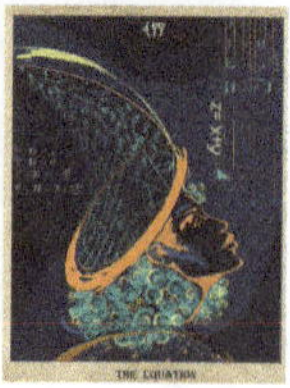

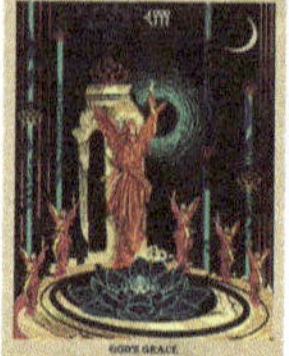

CIRCLE OF JUDGES

𒀭𒆜𒈾𒈨𒁹𒆠𒌷 𒁹𒄰 𒌋𒆜𒌋
𒐈𒀭𒌋𒐈𒀀𒈨𒆷 𒀺𒐈𒄰𒌋
𒉿𒌋𒐈𒆠𒁉𒄑𒐈𒆠𒆷𒈾𒐈𒐈 𒌋𒈨𒁉
𒆠𒐕𒋡𒐈𒃻𒌋𒐈𒀺 𒌋𒌷𒐈𒀭 𒌋𒁁𒃻𒌋𒐕
𒐈𒌋𒌷𒌋𒐈 𒌋𒈪𒁱𒈨𒃻 𒆷𒆢𒆠𒐈𒌋𒐈𒀸
𒌌𒐈𒐈𒌋 𒌷𒐕𒐈𒆠𒐈 𒅆𒋡𒐈 𒌋𒈪𒌋𒐈
𒐝𒐈𒌋 𒈪𒐈𒀭𒈪𒃻𒐈𒄑 𒀺𒐕𒐈 𒀺𒐈𒅆𒐈𒀺
𒐈𒌋𒌋 𒐈𒐕𒐨𒄑𒅆𒐈𒌋𒐈𒃻𒐈𒈪𒐈𒅆𒀀 𒀺𒐈
𒌊𒐕𒄑𒐈𒁁𒆠𒅆𒈪𒌋𒐈 𒀺𒐈𒐈 𒆠 𒀺𒐈𒈪𒐈

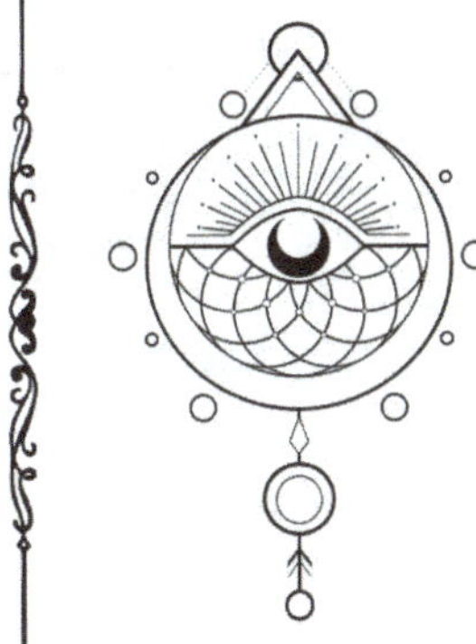

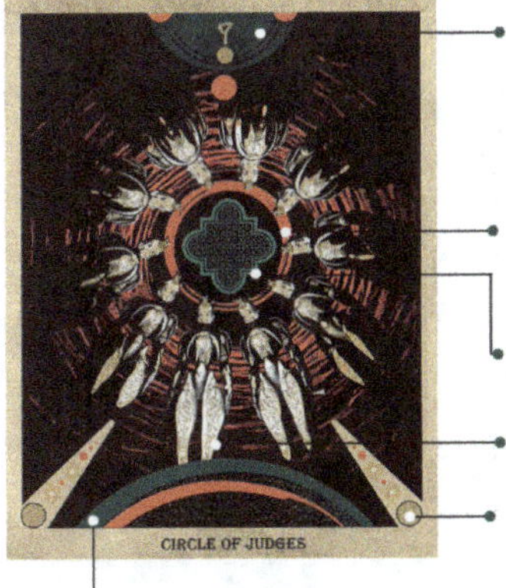

A semicircular design element that maintains the hirerarchy of elements. It is a point of intersection while forming a triangle, if joined to the circles in the bottom corners of the card, depicts a spotlight.

A joint circle that binds all the figurines as a single unit that shows their energies to act as one single point

The focal area that is a geometric pattern used to depict the idea of a ceiling over the heads of Circle of Judges.

The figurines - Circle of Judges.

Design elements to gather the viewer's attention to the figurines and focal point.

A design element that represents a platform/base or a stage.

TRADERS

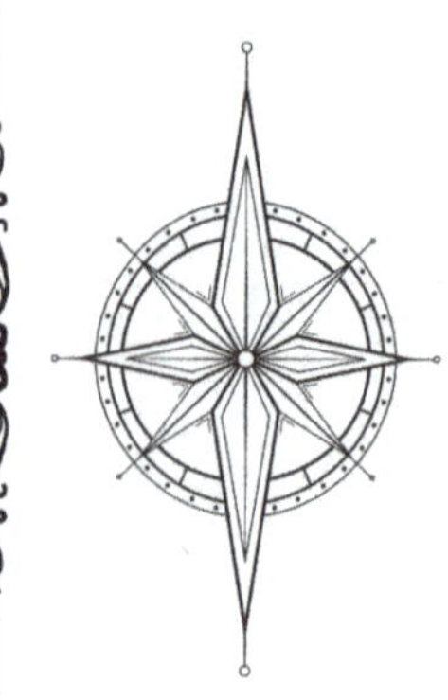

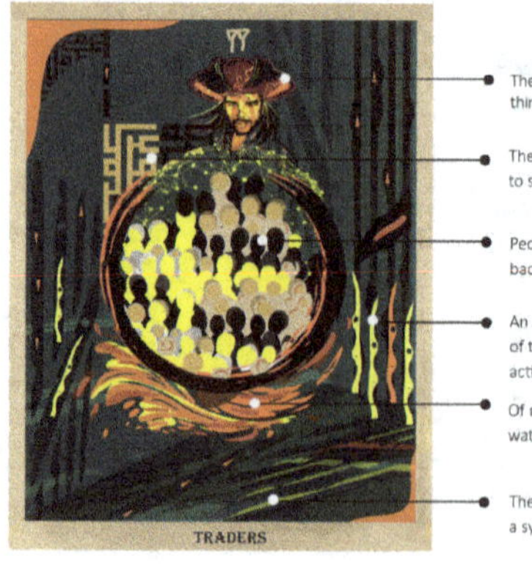

The Pirates that are the ones to take over certain things when the market is too rushy.

The abstract kufic patterns used as a design element to show the contemporary era.

People involed in trading with various departmental backgrounds.

An individual tally stick that represnts the weapons of traders and set of people involved into these activities.

Of related to the sea; Pirates,waves and running water and the nature of taking over.

The isometric top view of tally sticks, depicted in a symbolic manner.

COLLECTORS

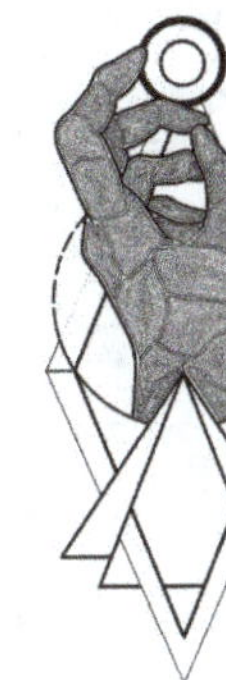

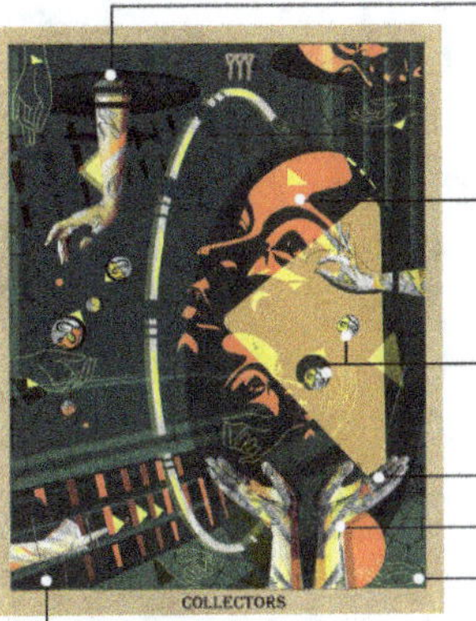

The most interesting design element of the card depicts a hand attached to the ceiling and dropping some of the collected downwards,turning the card upside down reveals the hidden meaning of this card; that collections are changing hands without even being noticed.

Reflection of a women with similar facial features.The two tonned hue depicts the vigilance of the collectors. As if they have one eye always open so as to get done with the purpose they have been made for.

The fetus encapsulated in a ball shapped womb.

The finger print patterns engraved on the hands of collectors that depict the whole process of collecting to be private and secured. .

The hands of Collectors are not directly touching the object of desire they collect.

The partially hidden hands of the collectors.

A design element to depict distance or perspective of the whole composition.

BURDEN BEARER

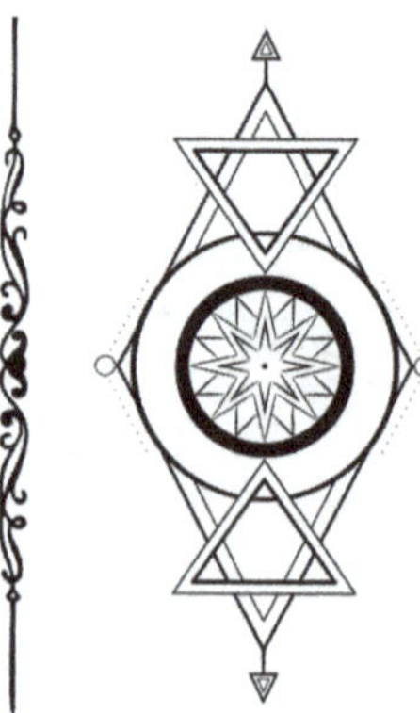

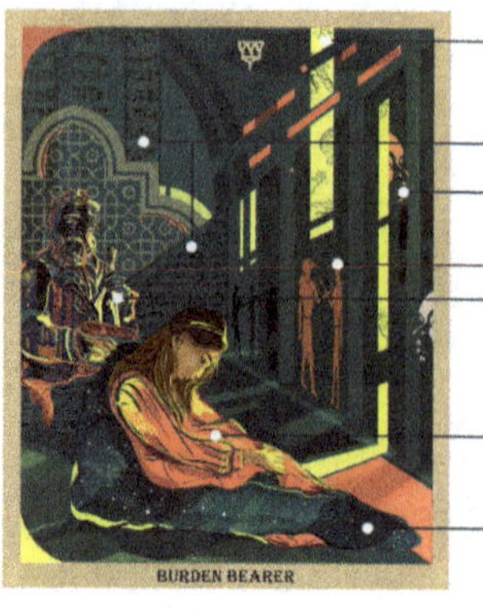

- Glass panels to let in light of hope inside the dark hall where the burden bearer is sitting and seeking forgiveness.

- Panels that depict ancient messages.

- The Collectors icons.

- Crows/bird shaped enlongated human like figurines on the wall panels in the background so as to link the relevance of the story and concept behind.

- The Mystagogue sitting on a higher slab, looking at the Burden Bearer.

- The Burden Bearer sitting on the floor with her head held down as a result of deep guilt and grief.

- The blanket covered with the galaxy pattern depicting the eternal blackness of the abyss of space and time.

THE AKASHIK

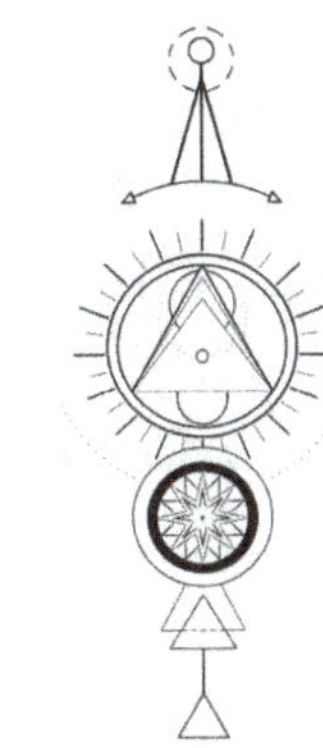

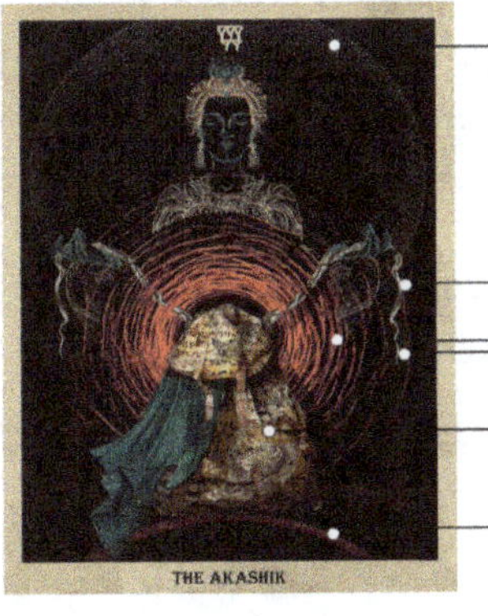

Two shaded dots depict the multi dimensional universe. The white dots also reflects the vast spectrum of stars in the dark.

The straps of the bag are held strong by imagionary positive universalenergy.

The red circular design element represents a black hole that vacuums in all materials. But the backpack with its Message of Rubies has the energy to stay where it is.

The arch in the background encapsulation the whole composition into it.

The backpack representing the ancient messages and a piece of The Akashik is sliding out from underneath the flap.

The curved surface is ought to be made as a base of the whole composition

PROTECTORS (Z)

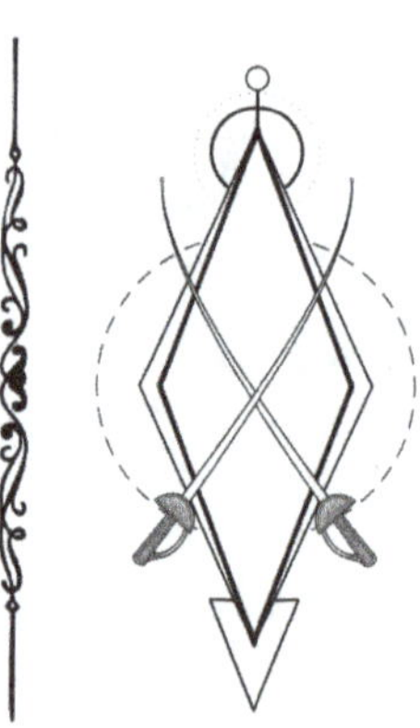

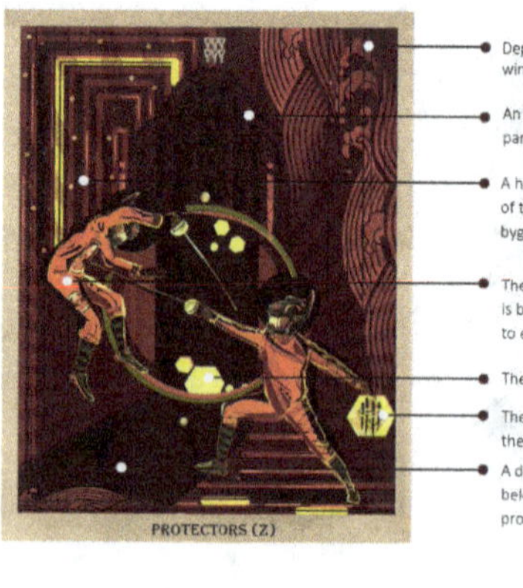

Depiction of waves of elements of life , be it fire;water; wind or even ether.

An arch encapsulating geometric patterns as a part of design.

A hallucinating backdrop to seperate the two parts of the canvas and so as to denote this as a space of bygones with the addition of stars.

The attacker; the one fighting from the other end is being set to the outer space whilst hindering him to enter the Precious sanctury.

The precious, gold, diamonds and other valuables.

The iconography of Nephilem,being protected by the protector.

A dark passage which may lead to the precious belongings that the protectors are trying to protect.

HUNTERS

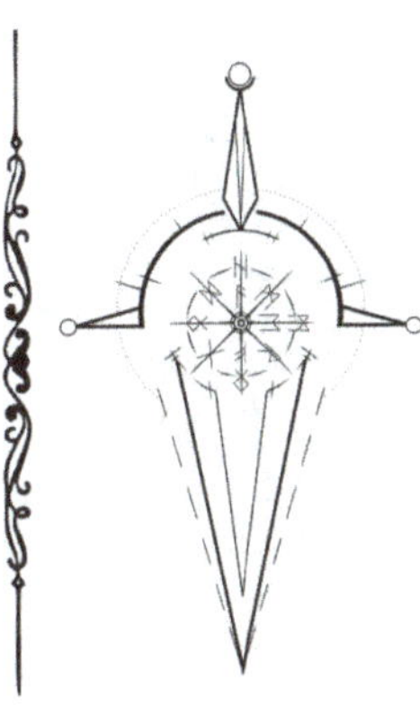

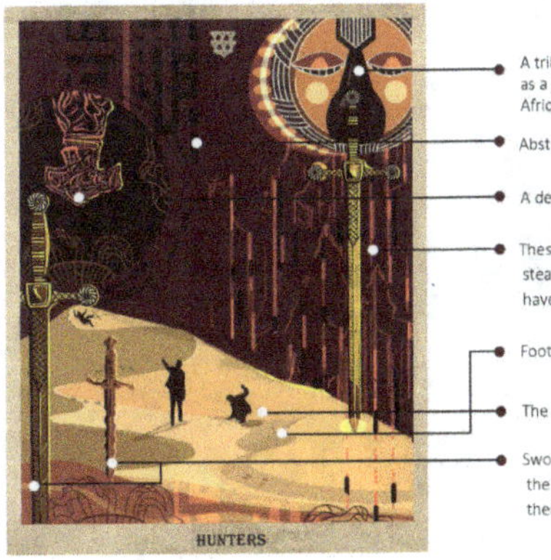

A tribal mask to cover the face of an individual as a hunter that originates out of a blend of African patterns.

Abstract kufic script used as a design element.

A demarcation of the tattoo of Seth, the Hunter,

These thin vertical lines are the expression of steady rocks standing in the background to have a perspective towards era.

Foot prints of the hunters on the sand dunes.

The hunters hunting on the way.

Swords standing straight reflect the tools that the hunters might be using as a protection on their way through the evil.

CROWS (Y)

"sin dines on its will" —

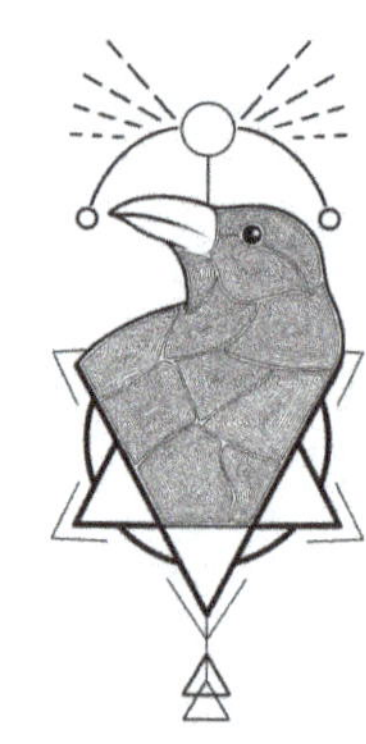

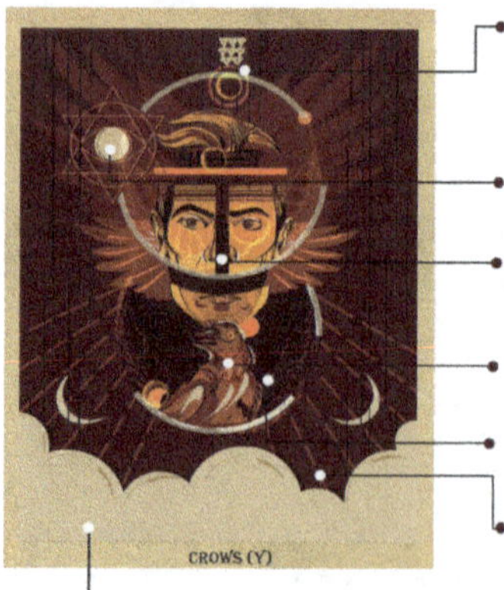

The dual circular ring shaped element that denotes the multi-directional nature of the crows character in the Eternal Game. It also represents a cycle from which the whole composition begins.

Six pointed star encapsulating an eye that denotes the eye of a crow.

The division shows the hierarchy of design in which it makes the crow the focal point of the card.

The Crow itself to partially depict the concept of this card,

Dark space denotes the crow as being one of the enemies of the nephilem.

Perspective lines to add a depth and focus to the composition.

Clouds are illustrated to depict the heights/concept of the crows and their active space and time.

OWLS (X)

"sin dines on its will" – 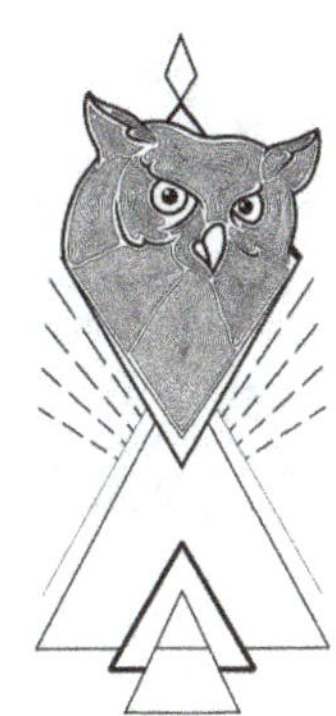

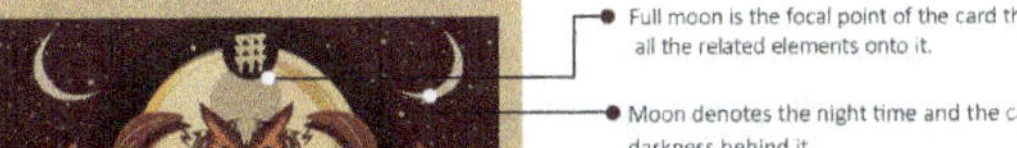

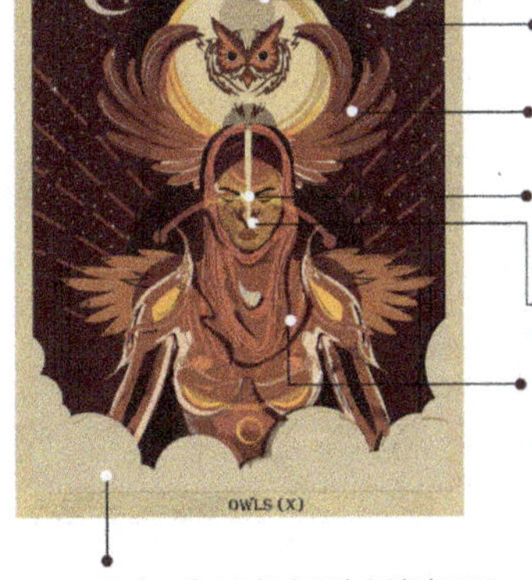

Full moon is the focal point of the card that hangs all the related elements onto it.

Moon denotes the night time and the cavity of darkness behind it.

The empowering wings of an owl.

A balancing design element that somehow shows the vibrant emergence of the oel out of it.

The physical attributes of the owl are added to the character to link it up to the whole concept of this card.

Veil shows the prevailing hidden nature/properties of the character i.e. owl.

Clouds are illustrated to depict the heights/concept of the owls and their active space and time.

MYSTAGOGUE

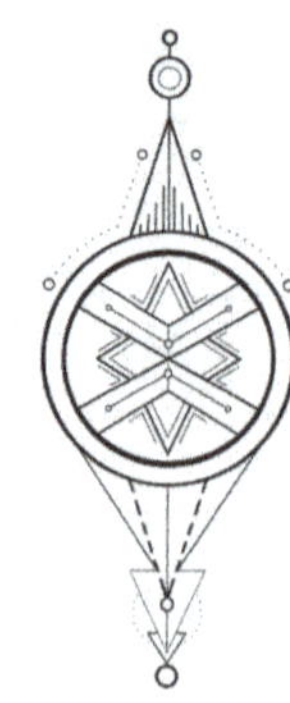

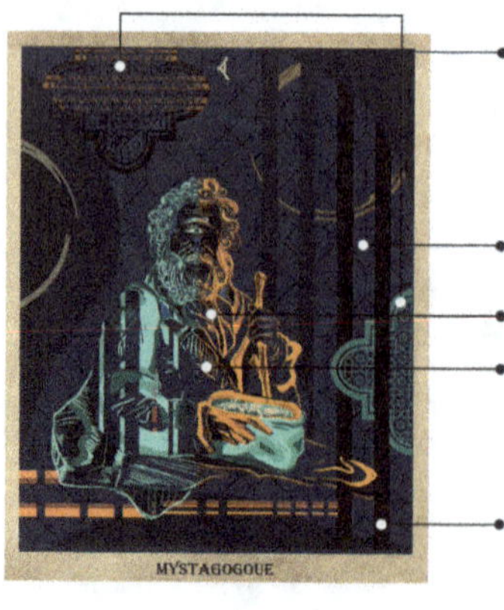

These motifs have been incorporated to depict a sense of peeking through the windows, something that allows the outer air (info/trends/knowhow) to get in and fill up the persona. These two colors are wisely chosen as they link these motifs to the half and half body of this humble old man / begger looking character.

The geometric pattern in the background to bind the composition.

One eyed man ; The Mystagogue.

The idea of having one eye could be depicted as one eye but two bodies or maybe as this soul is enlightened with God's grace. So the cyan-blue part is enlightened one and this light is further moving on to the other body part which is hued in orange.

The verticle lines are reflecting partial shadows or curtains behind which the Mytagogue appers.

NEPHILEM

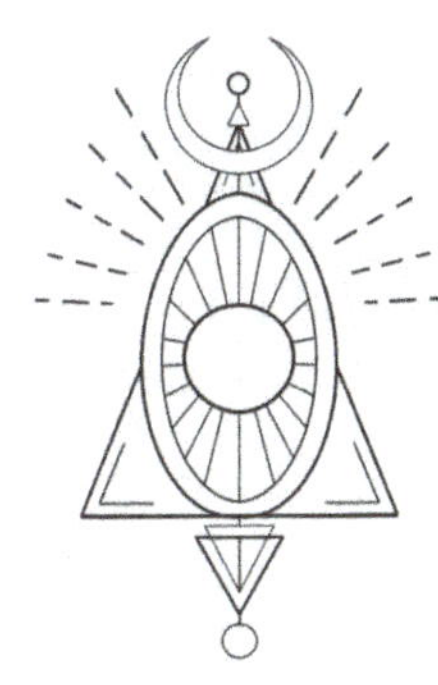

The universal icon with a power of holdong elements of universe inside of it .The planet, moon, mega star and sun are in the same orientation.

The oval shapped design element that holds the composition together, It is made to work as an orbit.

Geometric pattern in the backdrop.

The iconography of Nephilem.

The identical stone figurines with ancient finish (stone) which has several cracks on them. These figurines are holding the nephilem icon high up towards the central focal point of the composition.

The hands of stone figurines; that are not directly in contact with the slab on which the icon of Nephilem is placed.

The verticle lines are meant to depict the heights.

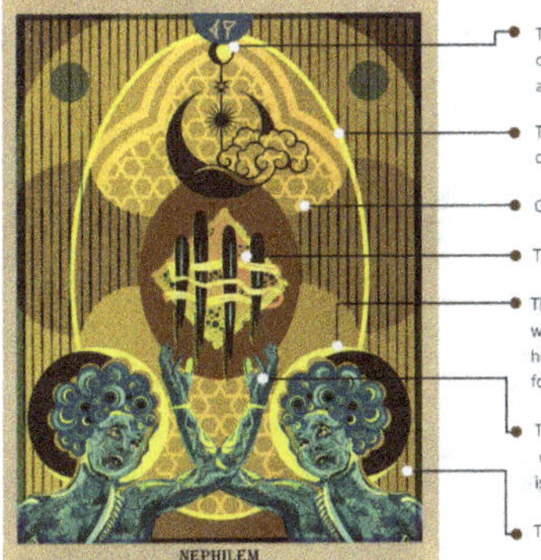

THE EQUATION

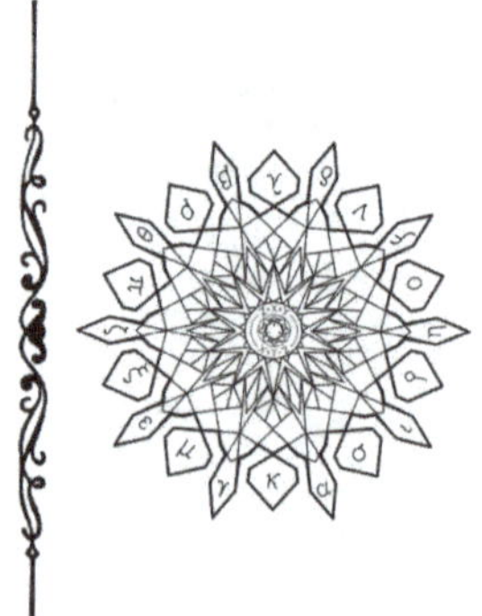

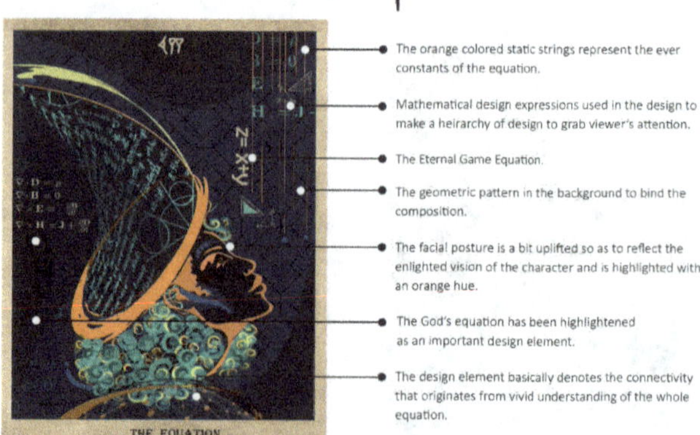

The orange colored static strings represent the ever constants of the equation.

Mathematical design expressions used in the design to make a heirarchy of design to grab viewer's attention.

The Eternal Game Equation.

The geometric pattern in the background to bind the composition.

The facial posture is a bit uplifted so as to reflect the enlighted vision of the character and is highlighted with an orange hue.

The God's equation has been highlightened as an important design element.

The design element basically denotes the connectivity that originates from vivid understanding of the whole equation.

GOD'S GRACE

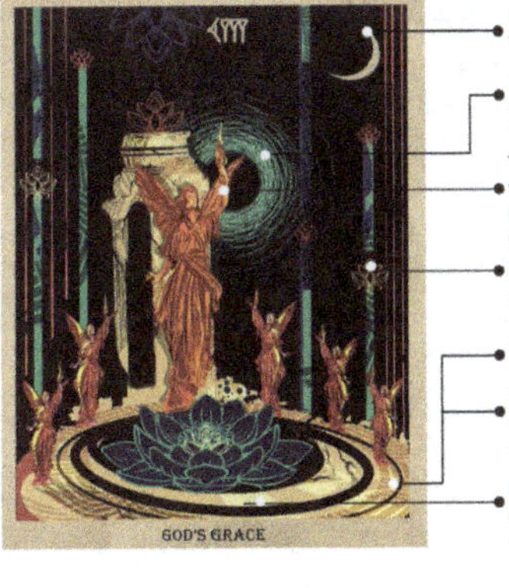

Half moon reflected by the resonating energy coming from the dark sun.

The dark sun which is letting a green hued positive energy from its surface so as to depict the positivity of the God's Grace.

The tall and heighted figurine holding a flamebeau, headed forward with chinup, is showing the highness and glory of God's Grace.

The vertical column like structures are meant to depict the heights.

The ancient built structure, more like the pantheon depicting the era.

The circular geometry of the platform on which these figurines are standing shows the oneness of the God's grace.

Lotus as the major element of design and concept is set on the base of a platform.

THE TIMELINE OF THE ETERNAL GAME

1930's – Theft of new-born babies begins as the Spanish Civil War ends. It is the ideological practice of stripping Franco opponents of their children to suppress the opposition.

1943 – An individual from a well-known family in Spain decides on a process that is more thoughtful and structured. The first philanthropic organisation, Manibus is created to facilitate the practice.

1950 – A disparate and enlightened group called *The Peers* oversee *Manibus* as the practice changes to focus on families seen as morally deficient. A network of officials including doctors, nuns, priests, and government officers are enlisted to administer the process of sourcing and distributing children for the Franco-regime.

1952 – An African nun in Bujaraloz Hospital meets a mother whom she believes has an elevated soul. She organizes an interview to introduce the woman to *The Peers*.

1953 – Aristocratic families in the nun's homeland of Spanish Guinea, become enamoured with the possibility of seeking _God's Grace_ through children. The ideology practiced by nuns under the noses of *Manibus* officials.

1956 – In Spanish Guinea, _The Collectors_ form to work with *Manibus* to create close ties with influential families, expanding their sphere of ideological influence to Spain. They aim to collect children whom they believe embodies _God's Grace._

1959 – The people of Spanish Guinea was given citizenship by El Caudillo, Francisco Franco of Spain. Using a formal network of kapok tree farmers, priests, and port personnel shipping begins of children from mainland Spain off-shore to newly formed Equatorial Guinea.

1960 – A Franco era priest, known as the *first priest* in Equatorial Guinea, continues his studies as he travels to Tamil Nadu, India to uncover a sacred mystery, a blanket that writes itself in an ancient language. During his journey, the first priest comes to understand there are 7 'marked ones'. He returns to Equatorial Guinea with the blanket, gives it to Manibus who fund his journey.

1961 – The *first priest* uses ideology to begin a blood quest to find _Nephilem_ descendants and human traffic them to _Collectors_ who fund his venture in return. The first _Traders_ come to the fore as intermediaries in the economy.

1963 – To move up the society ladder, an ambitious _Trader_, rumoured to be a witch from Trasmoz, has been caught selling a fake _Nephilem_ child, begins a secret affair with a _Collector_ .

1965 – After witnessing the wonder of the *Sacred Mystery*, the founder of Manibus struggles as *The Peers* reach an agreement to protect the entirety of _God's Grace_ within the sacred mystery as revealed to all of them. As a concession to forming the _Circle of Judges_, the founder initiates the first priest as the first _Mystagogue_, their truth now revealed to all judges. Meanwhile, the union of a _Trader_ and _Collector_, bears fruit, the eldest of the Moirae.

1968 – The kapok tree appears on the Coat of Arms and the flag of Equatorial Guinea as the second girl of *three-who-are-one* is born.

1971 – Equatorial Guinea, under a lunar eclipse in August, the *sacred mystery* known now as *The Akashik* is lost for 3 years. These years later become known as The Great Contemplation - Periya cintaṉai பெரிய சிந்தனை

1974 – A pair of former martial arts students meet a _Mystagogue_ in Tamil Nabu, India who is found with _The Akashik_. On it, is an inscription called *The Message Of Rubies*. Before dying, the _Mystagogue_ passes the blanket to a _Burden Bearer_ with instructions.

1975 – In the Tsingy Rock Forest, training with a cinquedea dagger, the former martial arts students now train a crack team of fighters on the razor-sharp rocks as the first _Hunters_. Their mission is to never lose track of _The Akashik_ and seek the purpose of those who wish to harness _God's Grace_.

1979 – The youngest of the Moirae is born in west Africa in poverty 20 kilometres from a diamond mine. The first enemies of the _Nephilem_ ideology appear on _The Akashik_ as the first true Nephilem is found using the dragon trail. All the Moirae unite in Trasmoz, Spain.

1980 – A _Burden Bearer_, a keen mathematician has a revelation of an _Equation_ that will come to define _God's Grace_ for others to come. _The Akashik_ defines the enemies of the _Nephilem_ as _Owls and Crows._

1981 – One of the _Protectors_ as defined by _The Akashik_, cannot help the first _Nephilem_ avoid being taken by _The Collectors_ and trades their fate for that of burdening _The Akashik._

ETERNAL GAME
SACRED GEOMETRY

CIRCLE OF JUDGES

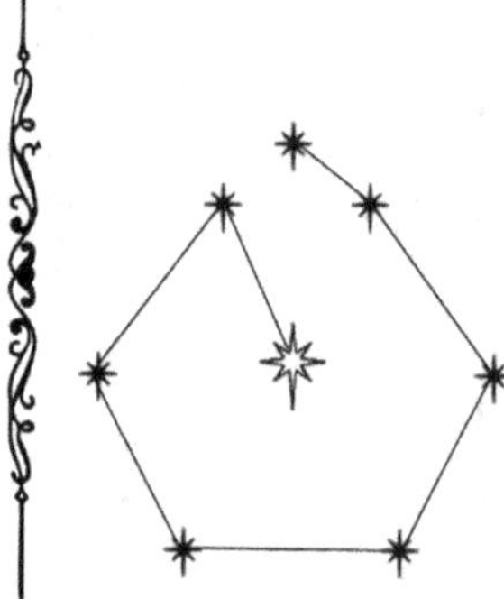

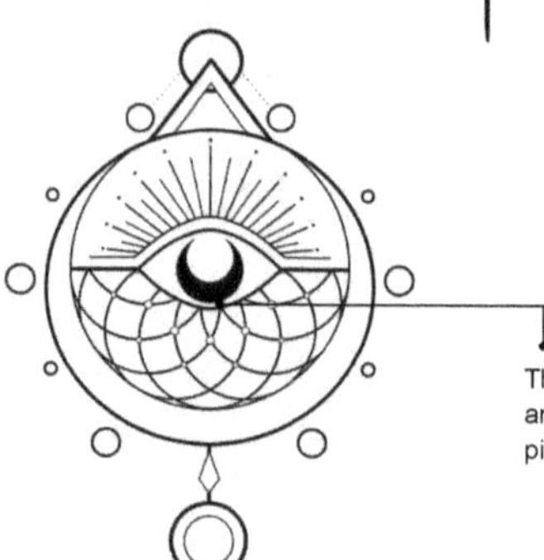

The eye represents Enlightenment and the Truth. Circles around this piece represent the Judges

TRADERS

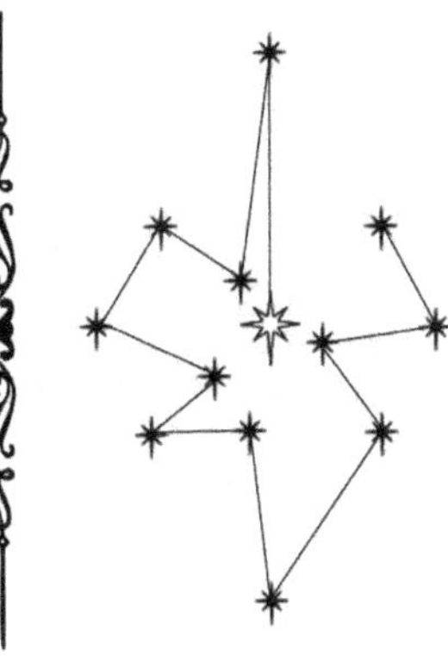

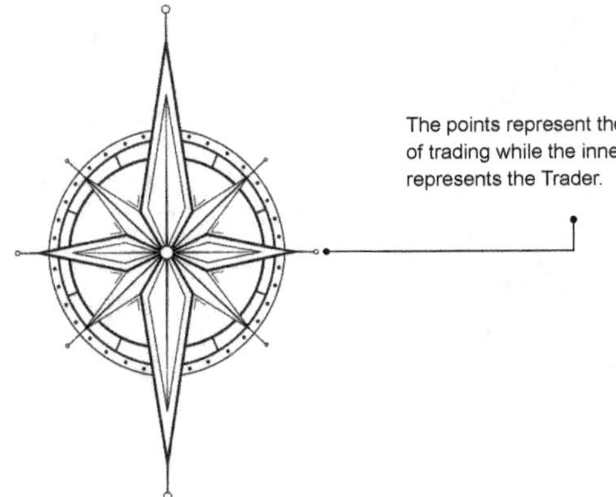

The points represent the act of trading while the inner circle represents the Trader.

COLLECTORS

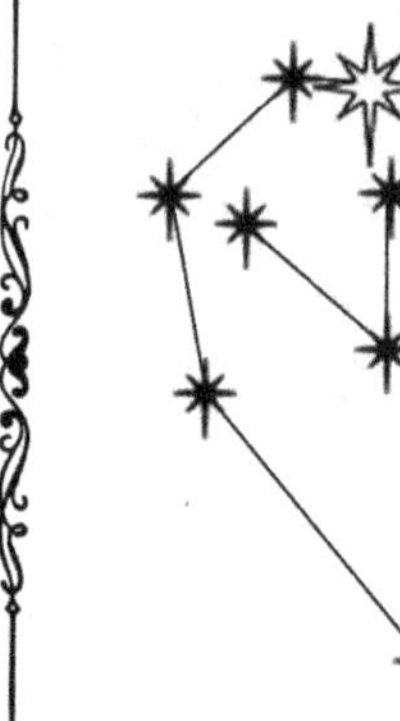

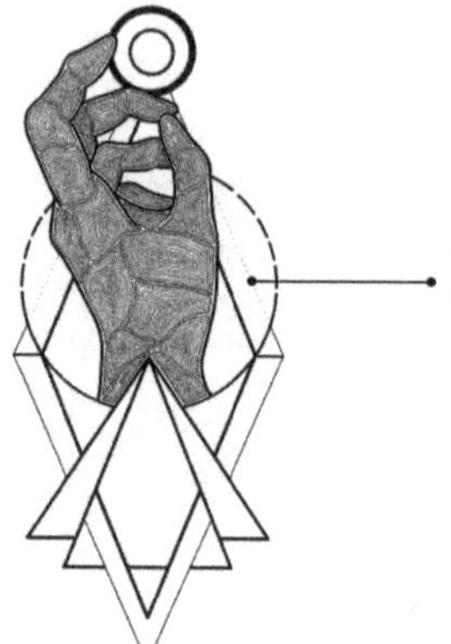

This is a literal concept – the hand collecting a 'trinket'.

BURDEN BEARER

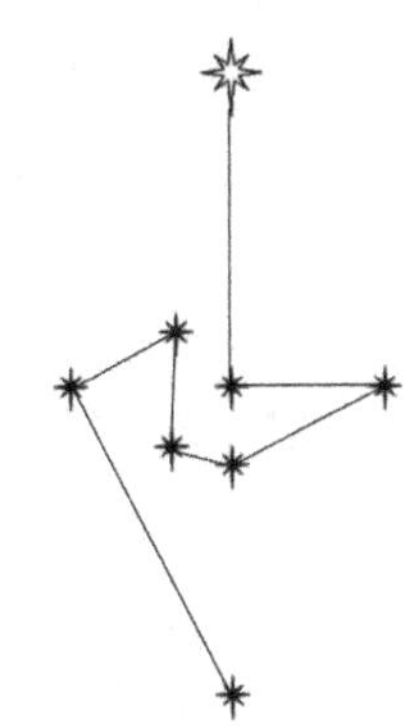

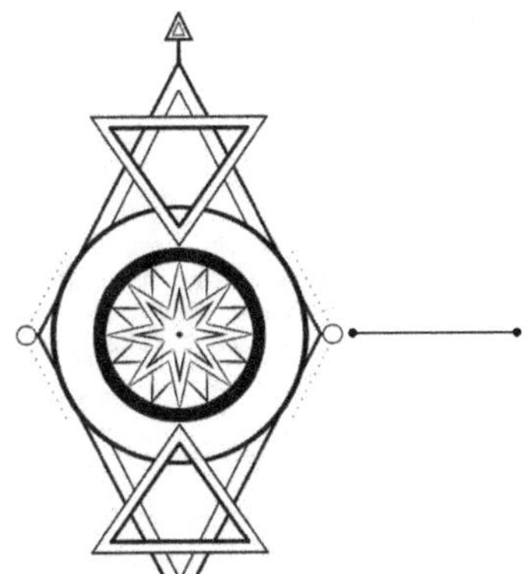

The star in the centre represents the Blanket of Stars, same symbol seen on The Akashik.

THE AKASHIK

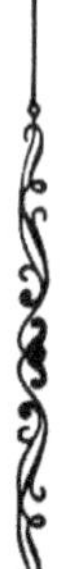

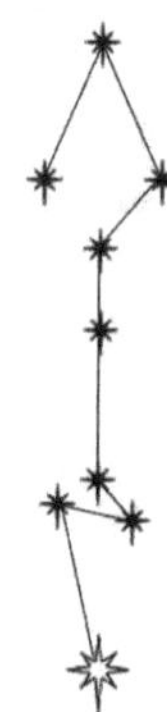

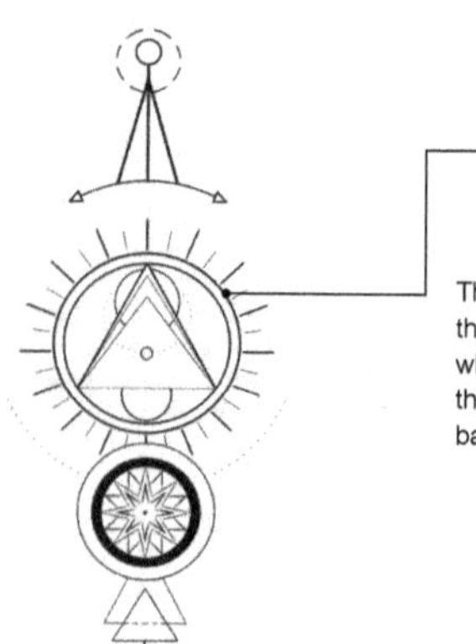

The main/ bigger circle represents the keeper or the main character, while the smaller circle represents the Blanket of Stars inside of the bag.

PROTECTORS (Z)

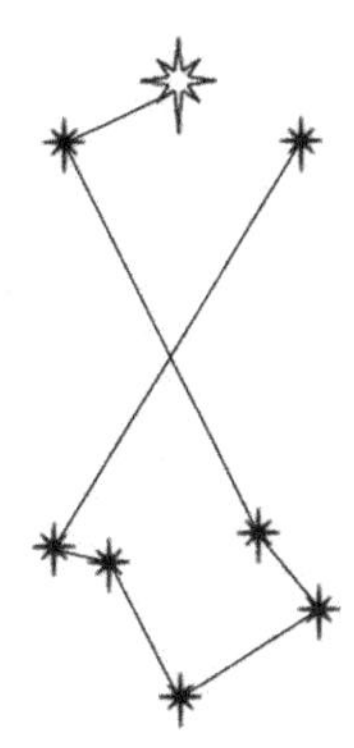

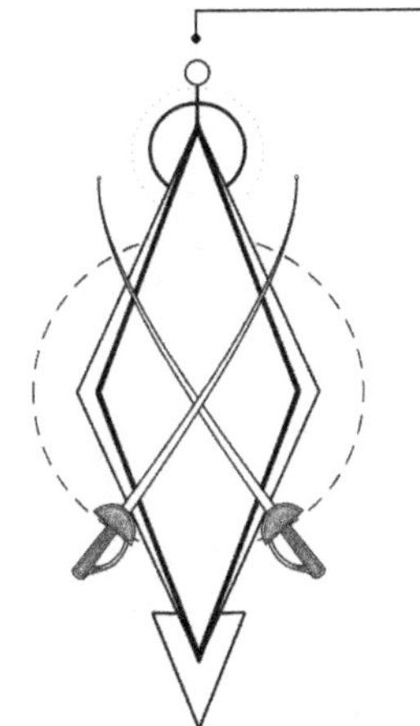

A more literal interpretation, showing the swords and a circle which represents the protection.

HUNTERS

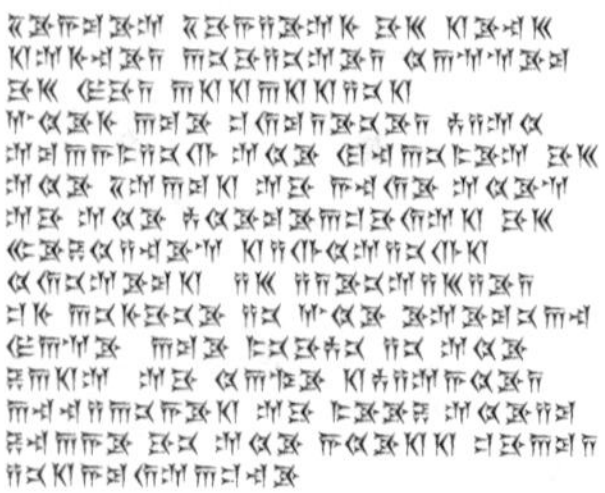

𒀸𒆳�𒅖𒀸𒆳�𒉌𒀸𒅗𒆳�𒆜
𒆳�𒆜𒀸𒁀𒌍𒀸𒂠𒌍𒀸𒁀𒍅𒍏𒀱𒄿
𒀸𒆜𒊭𒀸𒁀𒌍𒆳𒆳𒌍𒆳𒆳𒉌𒆳

𒌍𒍅𒀸𒆜𒌍𒅖𒁹𒊩𒅖𒌍𒀸𒁀𒄭𒉌𒍅
𒍑𒁹𒌍𒊓𒌒𒀱𒌍𒍝𒍑𒌍𒅖𒀸𒆜𒀸𒅖𒌍𒀸𒊓𒍑𒀸𒆜
𒍑𒌍𒀸𒆜𒌍𒌍𒆳𒆳𒁹𒍑𒌍𒀸𒊓𒌒𒀱𒍑𒍑𒀸𒌍
𒍑𒀸𒆜𒍑𒍑𒀸𒆜𒊭𒍑𒀸𒆜𒁹𒀸𒌍𒌒𒀸𒍝𒀱𒌍𒆳𒀸𒆜
𒍝𒀸𒅖𒍝𒌍𒀱𒌍𒀸𒌒𒌍𒆳𒌍𒍝𒍝𒍑𒌍𒌍𒍝𒍝𒆳
𒍝𒍝𒀱𒌍𒆜𒁀𒆳𒌍𒆜𒌍𒀸𒍝𒍑𒌍𒌍𒆜𒀸𒊩
𒁹𒆜𒌍𒍝𒆳𒆜𒍝𒀸𒆜𒌍𒍝𒌒𒍝𒀸𒆜𒀸𒍑𒀸𒁀𒍝𒌍𒀱
𒍝𒌒𒀱𒌍𒆜𒌍𒁀𒆜𒄿𒍝𒍝𒊓𒅖𒌍𒍝𒌍𒍝𒀸𒆜
𒊓𒌍𒆳𒌍𒌍𒆜𒍝𒌒𒀱𒍝𒆜𒆳𒊩𒍝𒌍𒌒𒍝𒀸𒍑
𒌒𒀱𒌍𒊩𒍝𒍝𒆳𒆜𒌍𒆜𒄿𒆜𒆜𒆳𒍑𒍝𒀸𒆜𒍝𒅖
𒆳𒀱𒌒𒌒𒆜𒆜𒀸𒍑𒀸𒆜𒍝𒍝𒀸𒆜𒆳𒆳𒁹𒆜𒌒𒍝�
𒍝𒀸𒆳𒌒𒌍𒍝𒀸𒌍𒌒𒀱𒌍𒀸

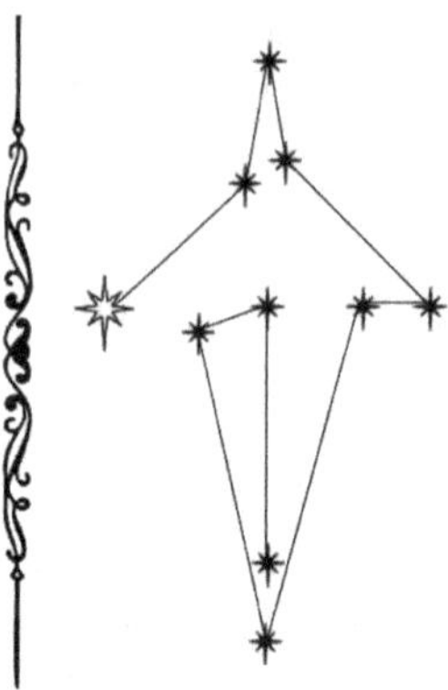

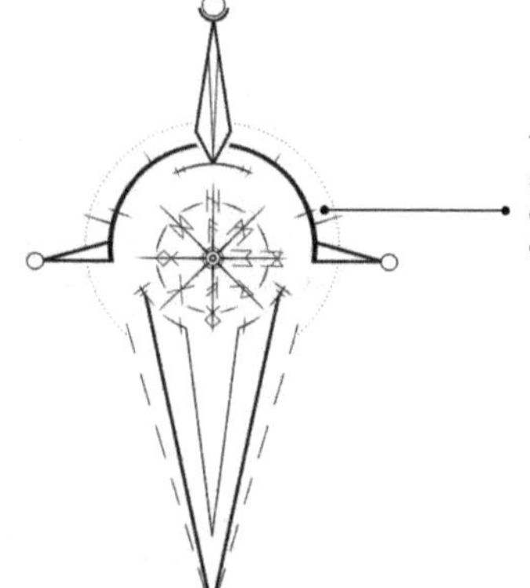

CROWS (Y)

"sin dines on its will" —

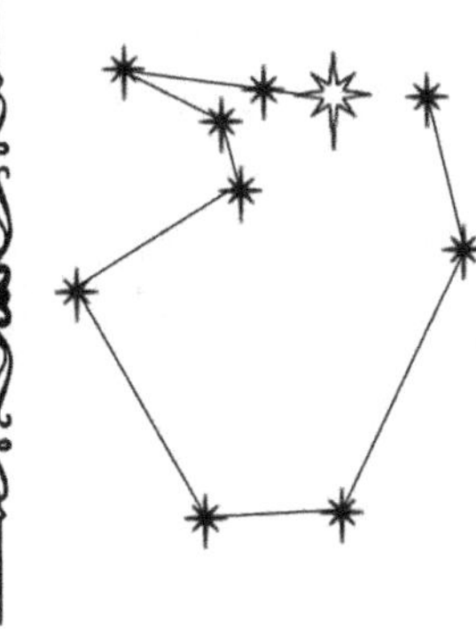

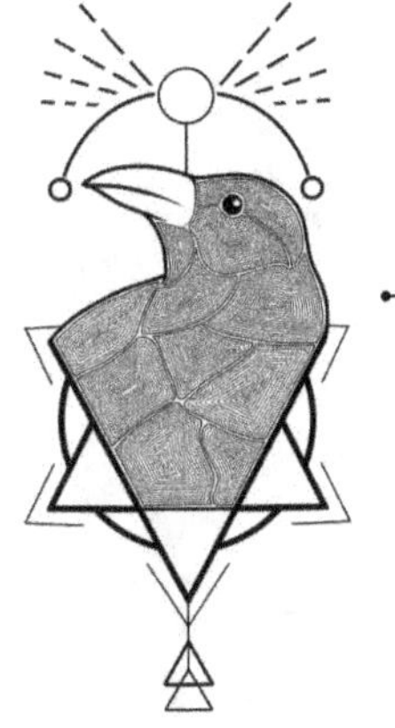

A literal interpretation of the crow with similar geometry that is featured in the cards.

OWLS (X)

"sin dines on its will" –

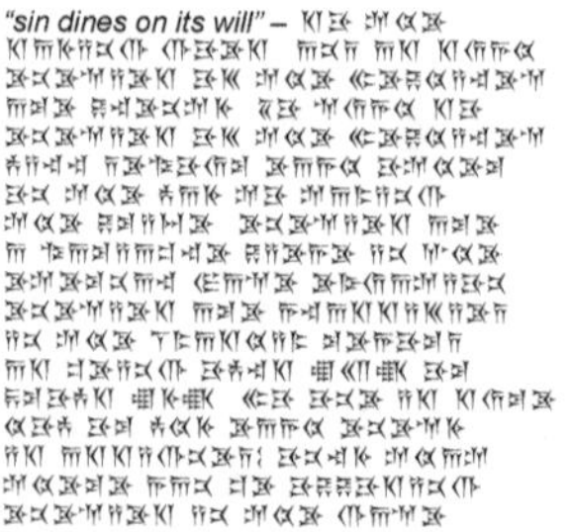

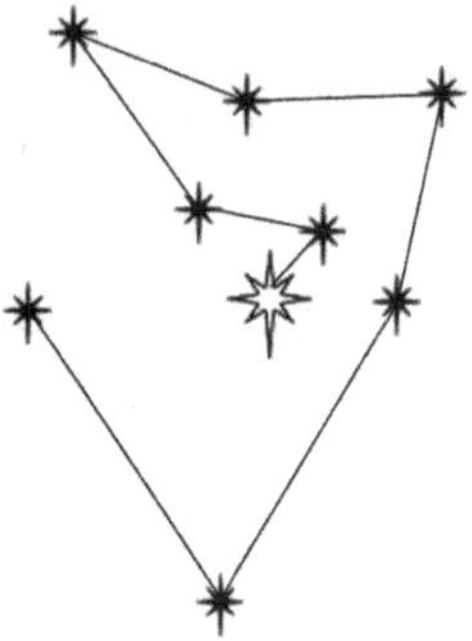

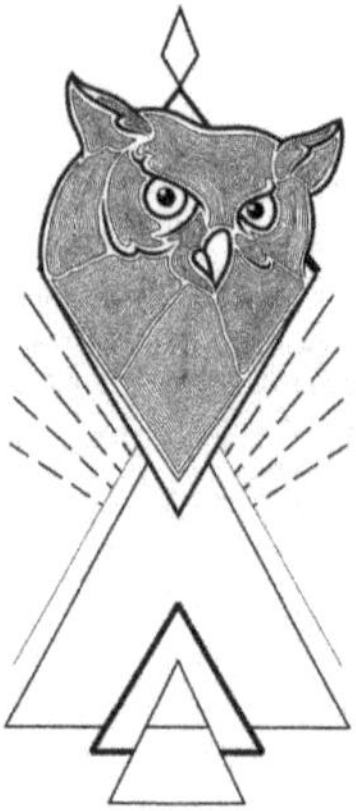

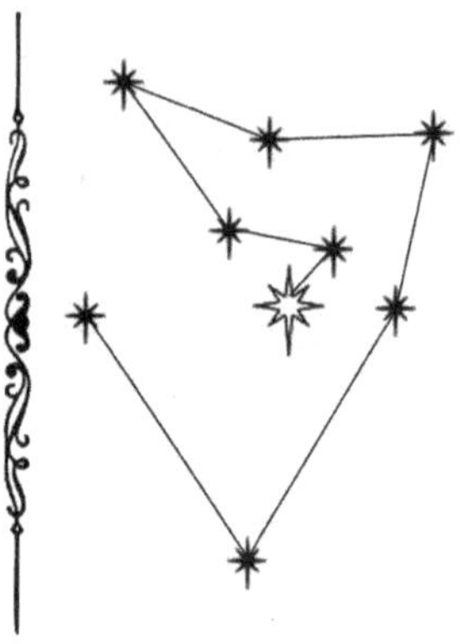

Another literal interpretation of the owl with similar geometry that is featured in the cards. I wanted to keep the Crow and Owl similar.

MYSTAGOGUE

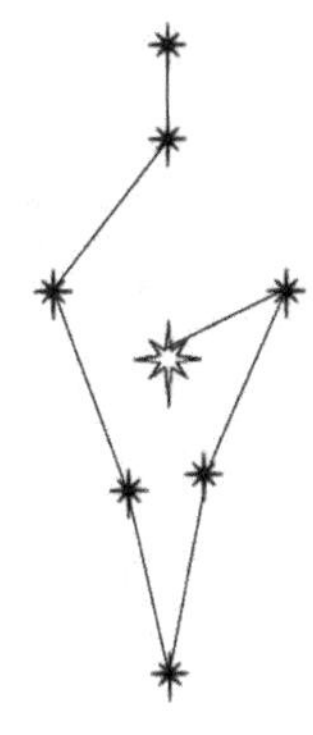

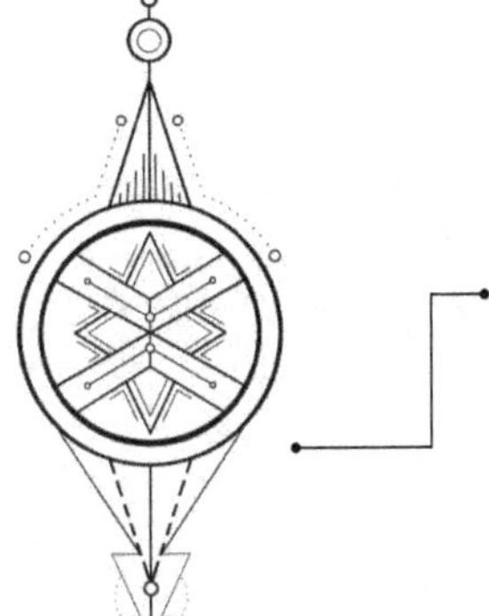

The circles and triangles in this piece represent the assignment from the Circle of Judges as the inner diamond represents the Mystagogue's good eye.

NEPHILEM

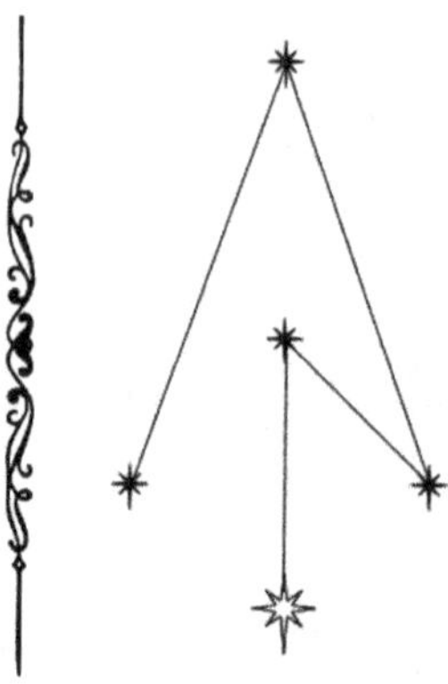

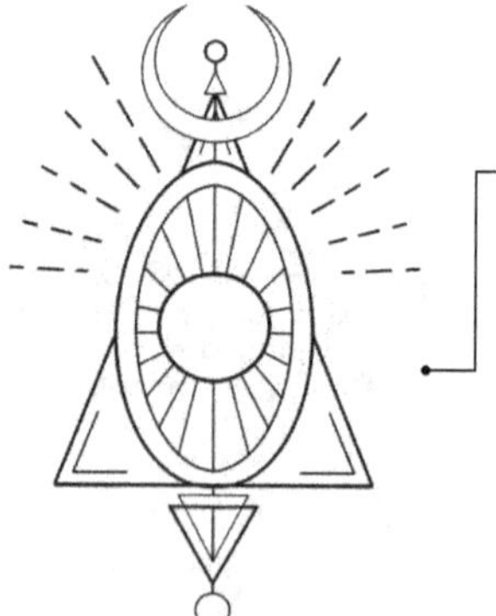

This represents the fallen Angel's and the concept of them being on earth with the ideology of the heavens.

THE EQUATION

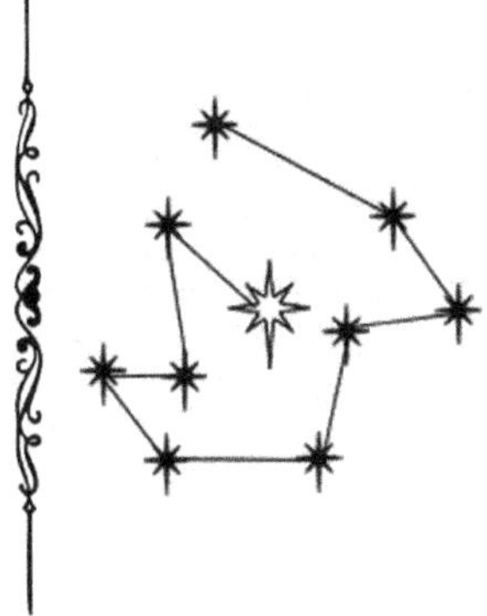

The geometry of this piece shows the precision of The Equation as well as has actual mathematical symbols on the outer edge. In the center there is The Equation of The Eternal Game ($Z=X+Y$ / $X=Y-Z$).

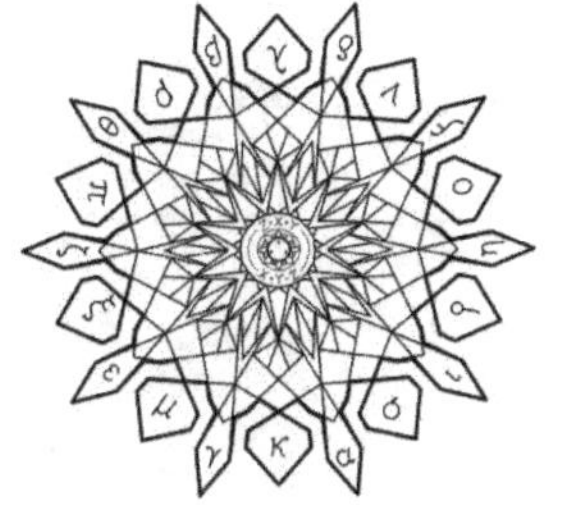

GOD'S GRACE

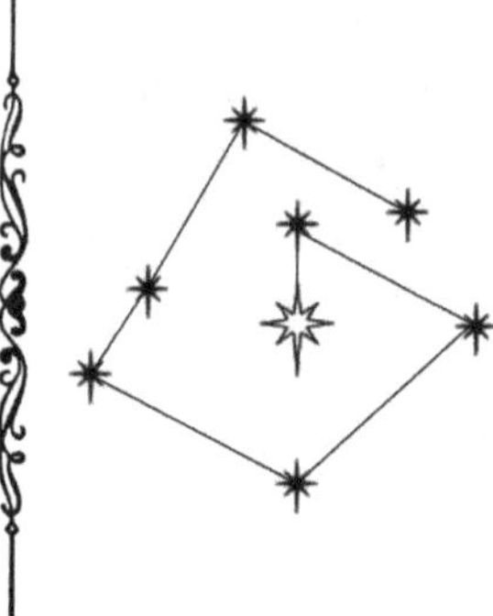

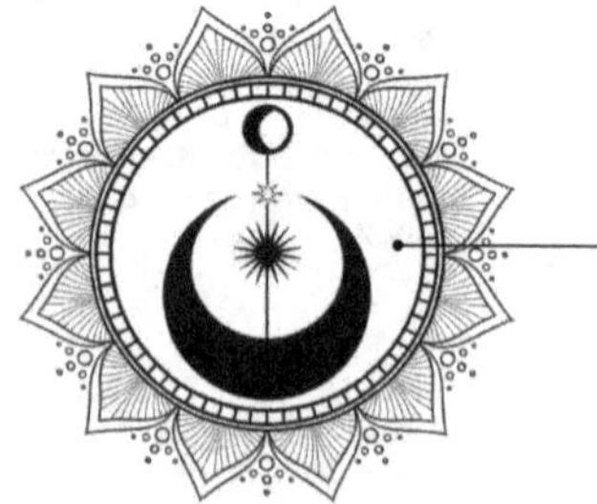

A geometric interpretation of the original card with the Lotus flower and The Eternal Game symbol in the center.

ASTROLOGICAL MAP
OF THE ETERNAL GAME

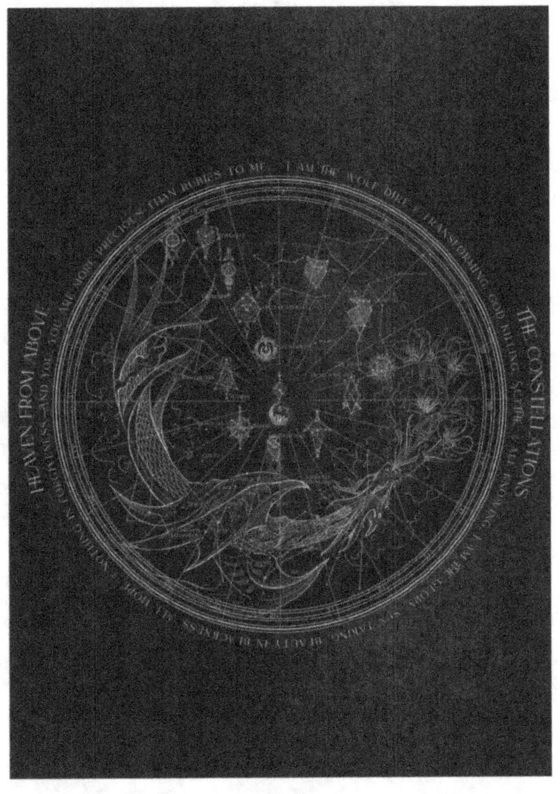

THE MESSAGE OF RUBIES

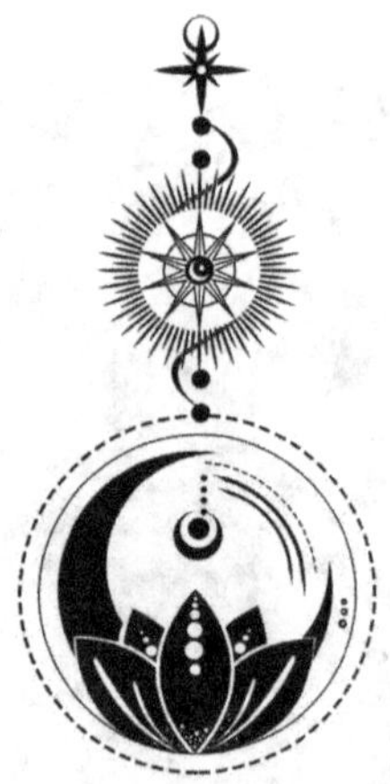

I am the wolf dire and transforming, god killing, Scythe, and all-knowing. I am the glory, sun-taking, beauty in blackness, all hope, and nothing in forgiveness. And you, you are more precious than rubies to me.

DRAFT ILLUSTRATIONS

Though the cards are numbered they certainly were not done in numbered order. The creation was a see-saw battle back and forth in the mind of Maham as she sat and thought on the concepts for a few months. The project started in October 2019, but stalled because Maham had been assigned and side-tracked to creating an illustration for *The Nephilem*. By the time of worldwide COVID-19 lockdown there was only one card complete, *Circle of Judges*. That sat as a kind of proof of concept until March 2020. Working from our homes, in enforced isolation, gave us both an opportunity to put our creative minds in synergy and make a proper start.

The following pages are snippets of our correspondence as we raced against the lifting of lockdown to complete the illustrations.

CIRCLE OF JUDGES

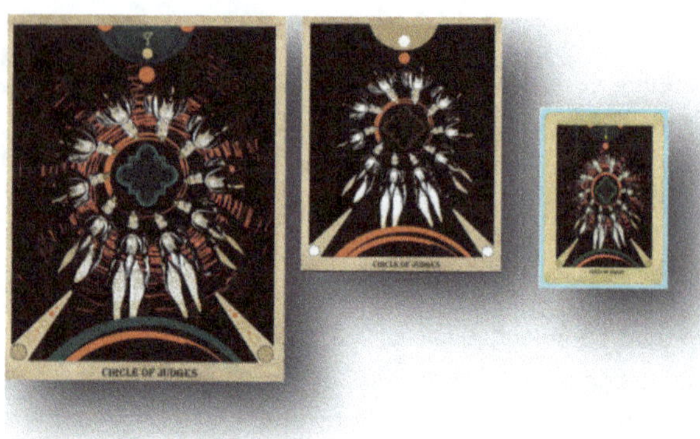

"The judges could be posed in a straight line arrangement and made to look like tall lean beings. But figure out your own way"
— Exquil

TRADERS

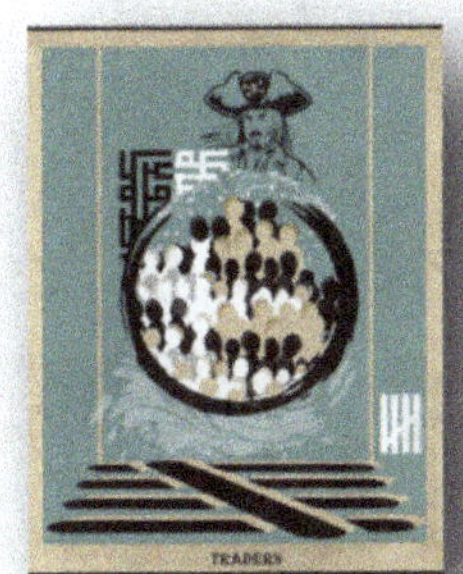

"*That pirate is chillin', why is he giving me the 'come to bed eyes'? Lol, oh my days! I'm being nudged-nudged wink-winked by a pirate. The card looks great Maham, cheers*"
— Exquil

COLLECTORS

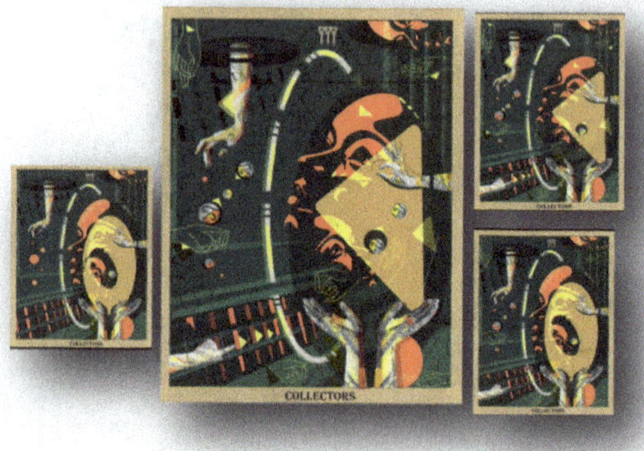

"I have an idea about Collectors — they like to possess things, hold on to them without necessarily touching them. So the theme here should be hands, lots of them."
— Exquil

BURDEN BEARER

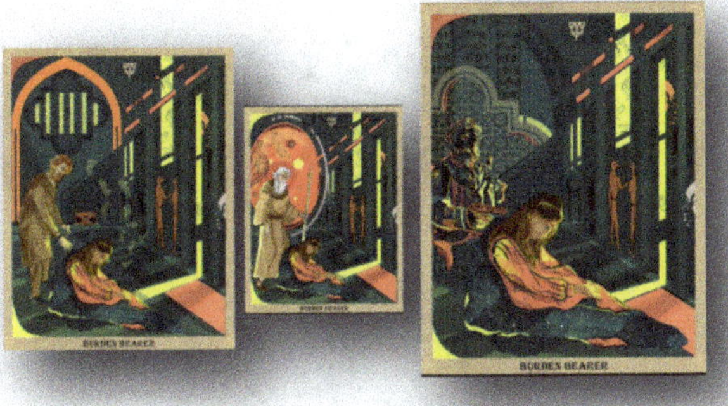

"*This scene needs emotional weight so body language will be very important. I think what would be great is if the passing of the burden happens in a city street. I particularly like it if this scene has graffiti on the walls.*"

— Exquil

THE AKASHIK

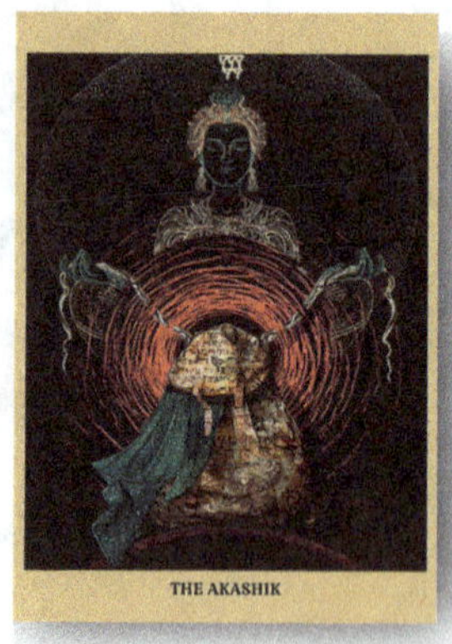

"…but I was thinking that a piece of the Akashik blanket could be sliding out from underneath the flap and on it written in Babylonian is a message. Or indeed the message could be written on the bag itself…you absolutely nailed this first time, very different, very cool"
— Exquil

PROTECTORS (Z)

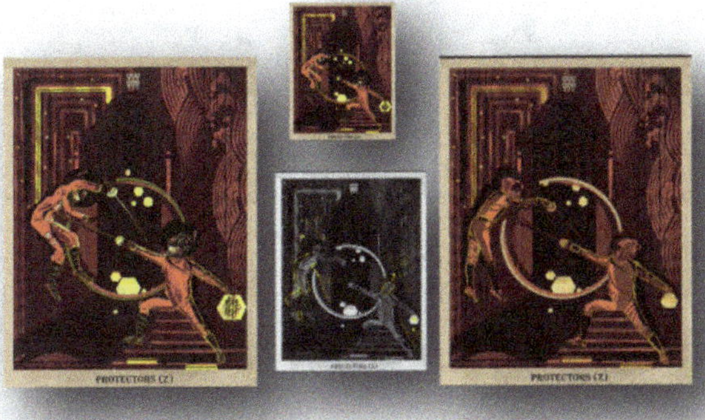

"*My recommendation for improvement here is the helmets of the dualist I think could look cooler. I think maybe more stylised. Perhaps futurist? Or maybe make a bit pointer at the back? I dunno, think of something to give them a bit of edge. And make the body language more impactful from the blows*"
—*Exquil*

HUNTERS

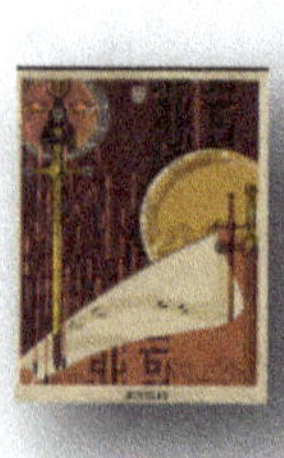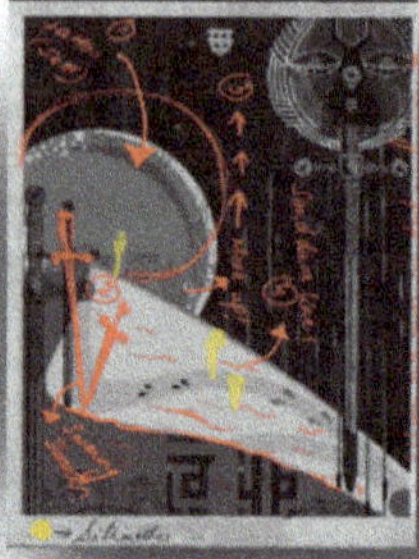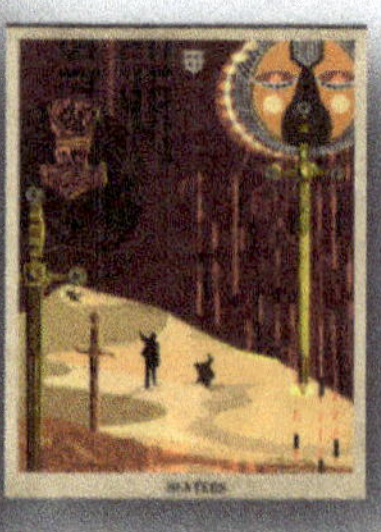

"ello Maham,
You know what, that sand dune is so much improved and adding the figures on there has added so much to it, not to mention the genius flipping of the image! Hunters is cool you know! Nice one. It is looking heavy now, it has got weight and authority now..
– Exquil

OWLS (X)

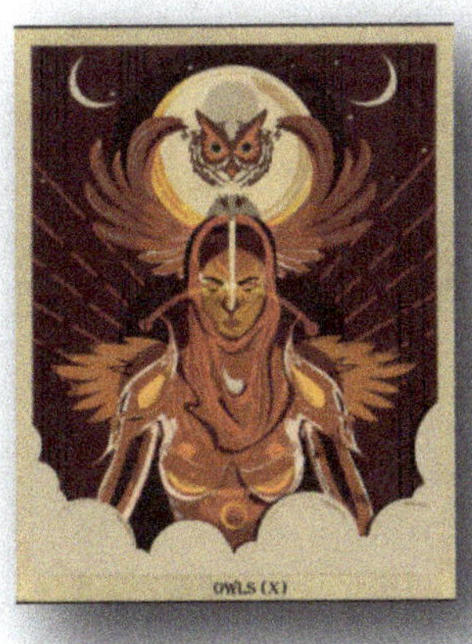

"I want a death mask with wings for Owls and Crows, and the capture of feminine grace...OMG, the quality keeps coming. I love the colour scheme! Superb imagination"
— Exquil

CROWS (Y)

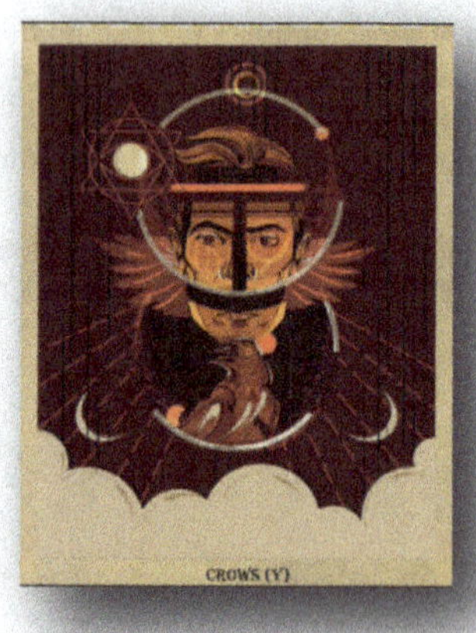

"I am happy with the outcome of recent cards except for "traders". That was the first one I worked on and pace wasn't picked up properly so I might want to change its look in terms of strokes and some color gradients…yes, you can expect these warm colors to be continued and ill use these symbols that you've suggested as needed in the design. Lets see how it comes out."

— Maham

MYSTATGOGUE

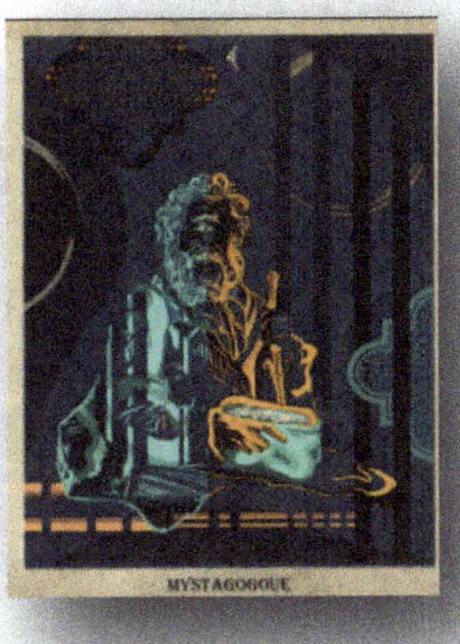

"The Mystogogue is looking superb. Did I tell you my idea for that came from a real-life encounter when I was a child? It was during a hot summer evening and we had the front door open as everyone did at that time, for those who didn't have air conditioning in their homes. Anyways, my mom was upstairs having a bath and a drunk man entered our home, a stranger, he walked in reeking of alcohol and asking me for money. Looking very similar to the guy on the card. He had one eye with a safety pin through the eyelid of the other eye. At the time I must've been only 5 or 6 years old so to me he was the real life bogeyman!"

— Exquil

NEPHILEM

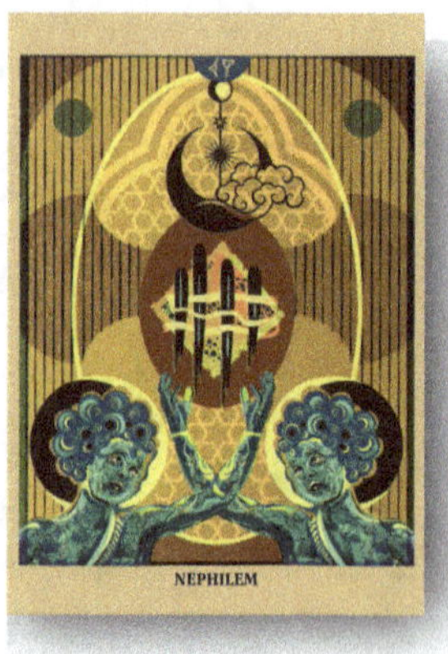

"I have this idea of them looking pieced together as if they're made from something else. I read, that in a field somewhere, there are heads meant for Mount Rushmore, like those heads I'd like to see these craked and aging."
— Exquil

THE EQUATION

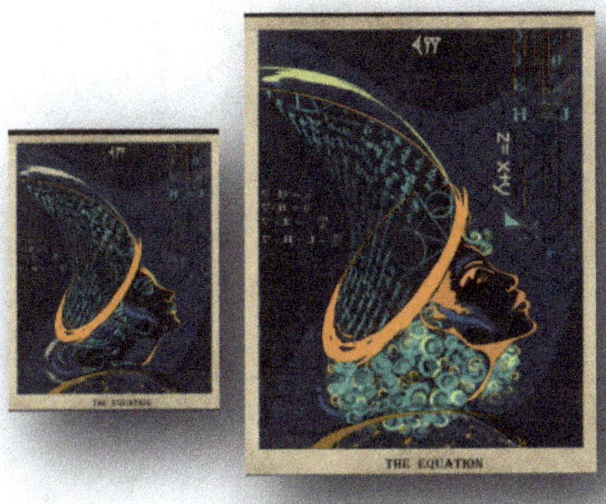

"But you must remember other numbers important to The Equation.

19 — all the cards summed. The number of Divine Order

11 — taking all responsibility for all peoples

13 - actions against God. In paganism, Molock demanded a

sacrifice of children

5 - symbol of balance, humanity and God's Grace

1 - entity concealed"

— Exquil

GOD'S GRACE

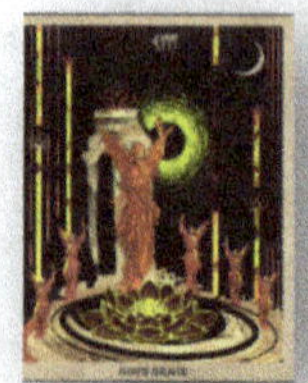

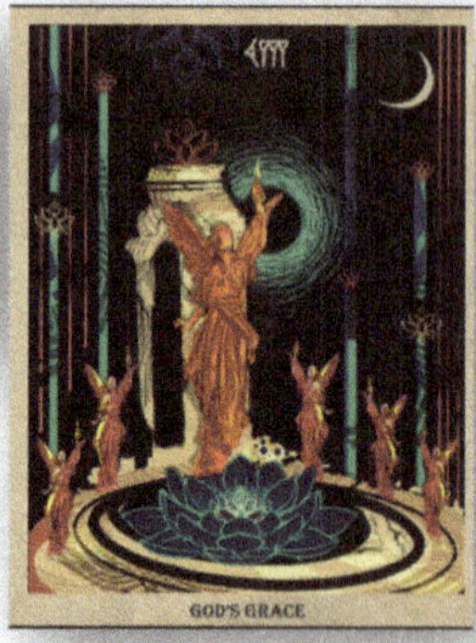

"*I worked on the traders and circle of judges while waiting for your brief and thinking deep how to capture the God's Grace card! I was nervous about this one when I started it. But then the flow was maintained thankfully.* "
— *Maham*

CONTACT SHEET
EXQUIL

We hope you enjoy the illustrations and will continue to support this original independent project by visiting our online portals to sign up for more information.

To find out more on *The Eternal Game* visit us online:

🌐 www.exquil.com

📌 Exquil Books

📷 Exquil Official

f Exquil Official

🐦 Exquil Official

✉ exquilbooks@gmail.com

#whatistheeternalgame

CONTACT SHEET
MAHAM

We hope you enjoy the illustrations and will continue to support this original independent project by visiting our online portals and sign-ing up for more information.

To find out more about *Maham Aziz's* art work visit her online:

mahamaziz.artgram
mahamdaneyal@gmail.com
Maham Aziz
Maham Aziz

CONTACT SHEET
CARMA

We hope you enjoy the illustrations and will continue to support this original independent project by visiting our online portals and sign-ing up for more information.

To hire *Carma Naude* for artwork contact her online:

✉ carmacalypso@gmail.com

🐦 CarmaCalypso

📷 witchcraftsarts

www.ingramcontent.com/pod-product-compliance
Lightning Source LLC
Chambersburg PA
CBHW061313140726
47998CB00006B/2367